Job Interview Secrets

Three16

Copyright © 2018 Three16

All Rights Reserved. This book may not be reproduced, in whole or in part, in any form or by any means electronic or mechanical, including photocopying, recording, or by any information storage retrieval system now known or hereafter invented, without written permission from the publisher, **Three16.**

CONTENTS

1. Preparing for a Job Interview
2. How Well Do You Know the Organization?
3. Improve Your Communication Skills
4. Confidence
5. Being Current
6. Are You Computer Literate?
7. How Well Do You Know Yourself?
8. Who is Your Role Model?
9. Job Interview Decorum
10. Job Interview Dress Code
11. The Organization's Instructions
12. Manage Your Time
13. Watch Your Grammar & Body Language
14. The Place of Experience
15. Job Interview Dos and Don'ts
16. Job Interview Pitfalls to be Avoided
17. Job Interview Etiquettes
18. Never Fear the Interviewers
19. Face to Face with the Interviewers
20. Sample Questions & Answering Guides
21. General Questions & Answering Guides
22. The Unwritten Rules in Summary
23. Expert's Helpful Comments

INTRODUCTION

In today's highly competitive job market, interview is an unavoidable hurdle every applicant must cross in the recruitment process of organizations that are hiring. As such, the need for a guide of this nature cannot be over-emphasized to any job seeker. This is coupled with the fact that most high institutions around the world do not teach job interview skills in their curriculum.

Having said that, have you ever failed a job interview? Experienced or observed that a thousand and one applicants do really pass job aptitude tests but only few successful candidates are usually chosen after oral interview?

You will rightly agree with me that so many applicants who having passed the tests, often miss out carelessly or ignorantly by failing to observe some rules of job interview.

It is in view of this fact therefore, that this job interview success guide is motivationally written for applicants who truly desire to pass their interview with ease and all smiles.

Please be encouraged to read this book with an open mind and I guarantee: you cannot but come across ideas, irresistible inspirations and creative words that will cause a positive change in your life towards success not only in your job interview but in life generally.

Suffice it to say that, with adequate preparation using this book in your hand and with God by your side, or whatever your beliefs, be inspired to study the instructions herein, imbibe and internalize the principles and do not hesitate to practicalize them during any job interview and your interviewers cannot but find you suitable for the prospective job that you seek.

I wish you best of luck.

Three16

DEDICATION

To Graduates & Job Seekers all over the world.

ACKNOWLEDGMENTS

My profound gratitude goes to God Almighty for the inspiration and wisdom of putting this book together for the betterment of the human species.

Indeed no one is an island of knowledge; as such, I'm indebted to all the sources and authors whom in the course of writing this book, I consulted their materials especially Ron Fry's "101 Great Answers to the Toughest Interview Questions."

1

Preparing for a Job Interview

"I will prepare and someday my chance will come." Abraham Lincoln

DEAR friend, do you know that job interviewers prepare before interviewing applicants? Likewise, as you plan and prepare for aptitude test, it is essential to prepare ahead of oral interview that usually take place after the aptitude test with a view to discovering your capability, credibility and suitability for the prospective job.

Therefore, while preparing for a job interview of any kind, you must be optimistic as: ***"Winning doesn't start around*** *you, it begins inside you and be informed that you will never possess what you are unwilling to pursue."* Mike Murdock observed. Of course, to get a job, you have got to start taking a step by preparing ahead believing that someday your chance will come. John Maxwell realized the importance of starting a task when he said: *"All accomplishment comes from daring to begin."*

And in line with the Abrahamic principle of preparation, be inspired to prepare ahead of your job interview bearing in mind that someday your chance will surely come. Remember that: *"The future belongs to those who see possibilities before they become obvious."* Ted Levitt encouraged.

Rule No. 1 >>>>Prepare and someday your chance will come.

Wisdom Keys and Action Steps:

"I will prepare and someday my chance will come."
Abraham Lincoln

"Those who fail to plan have planned to fail." Dr. Norman Vincent Peale

2

How well do you know the Organization you are Seeking Employment?

Now, let's use any corporate organization as a case in point in this guide.

> **Rule No. 2** >>>> *If you are seeking employment in any corporate organization, it is important to have background information about the organization's vision and mission and as well, familiarize yourself with general information about the organization.*

Find out the organization's website if they are online and just get clicking to know more about the organization's profile.

Please do not take this rule for granted as some interviewers under work pressure to interview many applicants may ask you simple questions about the organization, answering correctly will impress them and portray you as a prepared and serious candidate for the job. But on the other hand, failure to answer correctly, you may well be drawing the curtain on your chance to continue with the exercise.

Having prior knowledge and information of the organization's products or services and the position you will be interviewed for will no doubt help you immensely during the interview proper.

Wisdom Keys and Action Steps:

"It is more important to know where you are going than to see how fast you can get there." Martin Van bee

"You will never possess what you are unwilling to pursue." Mike Murdock

3

Improve Your Communication Skills

Communication is the life blood of any organization or human endeavor and job interview inclusive.

Why is communication skill important in job interview?

Undoubtedly, communication is the life blood of any organization or human endeavor and that includes job interview for that matter.

Improved communication shows your resources and what

stuff you are made up of.

So also, being an effective communicator will make your interviewers take you seriously, listen to you and engage you in a keen interactive session instead of the traditional questions and answers routine.

> **Rule No. 3>>>>Be an avid reader. Read voraciously and omnivorously. This will no doubt improve your communication skills and command of English Language.**

Wisdom Keys and Action Steps:

"Upgrade your skills. Update yourself. Develop your character. Set goals ahead of expected opportunities."

"Being an effective communicator means that your interviewers will take you seriously and engage you in dialogue."

"Success doesn't just happen, you set it in motion." Mike Murdock

"Don't just dream of great accomplishments, stay awake and do them." John Mason

4

Confidence

"One of the most powerful concepts, one which is a sure cure for lack of confidence is the thought that God is actually with you and helping you." Dr. Norman Vincent Peale

Why is confidence and boldness important in job interview?

- It is a state of mind that affects your interview positively or negatively.

- It is one of the basic qualities your interviewers desire to see you posses.
- Lack of confidence in oneself and ability is a breeding ground for low self esteem or inferiority complex: a feeling that one is less important, less clever or less admired than other people. This feeling makes some people aggressive and others shy. It is a negativistic and pessimistic mindset sometimes caused by illusion, ignorance, and poverty, wrong mental attitude, underestimating oneself and rating others above oneself. This must be consciously dealt with and rejected if your confidence must improve. Dr. Norman Vincent Peale realized the danger of this when he said: ***"A sense of inferiority and inadequacy interferes with the attainment of your hopes but self confidence leads to successful achievement."***

On the other hand, over confidence causes superiority complex: a strong and unreasonable belief that one is more important than other people. And this is usually motivated by illusion, prejudice and pomposity/arrogance! Ipso facto therefore, improve your self confidence with what I like to term "*self-equilibrium-complex*": a situation in which you and opposing influences, forces, etc are balanced and under control. Yes, imbibe the "Can Do spirit" and believe that you are equal to the task that may be presented to you by the panel of interviewers you may encounter. Have a state of mind in which feelings and emotions are under control.

Be confident, composed, relaxed, smile and feel at ease whenever you are face to face with your interviewers. They are not ghosts but human beings like you! (Smiles….)

Improve your confidence by improving your style of dress (not necessarily expensive or gorgeous dress), read inspirational, motivational and mind building books. Yes, work on your self esteem and physical appearance and invest in good clothes.
And before going in to face the interviewers, ease or diffuse tension by taking a deep breath in and out at least three times before going into the interview hall to face the interviewers. **It is normal to get tensed up before the interview; hence the above exercise is "vital essential".**

Above all, imbibe and internalize Philippians 4:13: ***"I can do all things through Christ which strengthens me"***. There is no self-confidence and self-esteem booster than that verse if you ask me. And I love the words of Lillian Hellmann when she said: ***"It is best to act with confidence, no matter how little right you have to it."***

Rule No. 4 >>>> Be bold, confident, composed, relaxed, SMILE and feel at ease whenever you are face to face with your interviewers.

Wisdom Keys and Action Steps:

"For God has not given you the spirit of fear, but of boldness, of love and sound mind." (Bible)

"Boldness in vision is the first, second, and third most important thing. He who dares nothing should expect nothing. " John Mason

"Believe what God said right in the face of all contrary sense knowledge and you shall have them." Joel Osteen

"In the race of life, only the confident wins the race." Anonymous

"I can do all things through Christ which strengthens me." (Bible)

"One of the most powerful concepts, one which is sure cure for lack of self confidence is the thought that God is with you and is actually helping you." Dr. Norman Vincent Peale

"Yes, be bold and strong. Banish fear and doubt. For remember, the Lord your God is with you wherever you go." Joshua 1:9 TLB

5

Being Current

"If you are not informed, you are deformed." Anonymous

As an applicant preparing for a job interview, it is essential to be aware of current happenings in your immediate environment, country and the world at large.

This is where most applicants concentrate their preparation on (current affairs) while ignoring some vital aspect of the life changing exercise.

No doubt, job interviewers normally ask some current affairs oriented questions with a view to discovering your sharpness, consciousness about the society you live in; the level of your exposure socially and whether you are in tune with the happenings in and around you, and the ever changing contemporary society we live in.

In connection to the foregoing therefore, make it a habit to listen to news reports daily on radio or television as well as newspapers regularly if you can; not just because you are preparing for a job interview, but to be more informed, educated, entertained, and for general self improvement.

I personally have experienced and practiced the principles herein, and was able to correctly answer a job interview questions because I was current and in tune with the current happenings back then. Buddy, it pays to be current!

Rule No. 5 >>>> Be in tune with current happenings. It pays off during job interviews.

Wisdom Keys and Action Steps:

"If you are not informed, you are deformed." Anonymous
"Never admit failure until you have made your last attempt; never make your last attempt until you have succeeded." Benjamin Disraeli

"Strong men are made by oppositions, like kites they go against the winds to rise." Frank Hern

"There is only one good, that is knowledge; and one evil, that is ignorance." Aristotle

"My people are destroyed for lack of knowledge." (Hosea 4:6)

6

Are You Computer Literate?

"Candidates who are computer literate have an added advantage." (Job vacancy catchphrase)

MOST job vacancies advertisements these days whether online, in newspapers or posters etc, normally add a rider thus: "**computer knowledge is an added advantage for this position.**"

Did you hear that? If yes, then what more do you need to hear to spur you on to learning computer basics if you are not computer literate as an applicant in this computer age and information advanced technology era?

It is in your own best interest to be computer literate if you are not. And always work towards increasing your capacity and try to be better than you were three months ago.

Rule No. 6 >>>> Make a conscious and deliberate effort to be computer literate if you are not.

Wisdom Keys and Action Steps:

"Change will not come if we wait for some other person or some other time."

"Pleasure in the job puts perfection in the work." Aristotle

"It does not take discipline to dream but it does take discipline to make those dreams real." John Maxwell

"If you spend your life inside waiting for the storms, you will never enjoy the sunshine." Morris West

"Always improve your capacity and make it a habit to be better than you were three months ago."

7

How Well Do You Know Yourself

"A sense of inferiority complex and inadequacy interferes with the attainment of your hopes but self-confidence leads to self-realization and successful achievement." Dr. Norman Vincent Peale

WHAT has self-realization got to do with job interview? Well, if you think so then, I have got news for you. Yes, self-realization really has everything to do with job interview. Do you know why? This is because most experienced job interviewers in recruiting organizations and Human Resource department of most recruiting organizations unfailingly ask applicants questions such as:

Can you tell me about yourself? Or tell me about yourself. Or what is it that you don't like about yourself? Can you beat that! And of course, it takes self-realization to answer such questions.

Please note that such questions are asked with a view to discovering one or more of the following about you: who you think you are; your self-esteem, intelligence, confidence, character, and if you are motivated; your strengths and weaknesses in relation to the prospective job.

Against this backdrop therefore, while answering question of that nature, always bear in mind that: *"The most effective person to point your finger at is you. Accepting responsibilities for your actions and inactions without wasting time on criticizing yourself are the hallmark of an effective person."* Brain Koslow advised.

Truly, you and I and all the interviewers inclusive all have our strengths and weaknesses, but it is self-realization and individual character, habit and ability in improving oneself that makes the difference.

Accepting responsibilities for your weaknesses, and showing willingness to improve yourself instead of arguing and giving unnecessary excuses to justify them is a right step in the right direction towards self-realization. Benjamin Franklin once said: *"He who is good at making excuses is seldom good for anything else."* And in concurrence, George Washington Carver opined that: *"Ninety-nine percent of failures come from people who have the habit of making excuses."*

Now, let's assume I was your job interviewer in a recruiting organization, and during the exercise I asked you this tricky question: **what is it that you don't like about yourself?** And you quickly answered without thinking about the implication of your response by mentioning one or more of the following: anger, lies, argument, stealing, fighting, and drunkenness; etc, or you introduced any negativity that could hamper the progress of the prospective job. Do you think I would find you suitable for the job? Smiles...... Of course, your guess is as good as mine.

By that very fact therefore, your discretion, and strong sense of reasoning and sound judgment is needed in answering such a put up job (or tricky question). And be informed that the interview room is not a confessional wherein you go to confess your sins to a priest. Don't worry because you will find more of such questions and answering guides later on in subsequent nuggets.

Now, who are you? Proverbs 23:7 categorically states that: *"As a man thinks in his heart, so is he."* And James Allen affirmed by saying that: *"A man is literally what he thinks."* And I concur absolutely.

Think greatness and pay the price of the hard work and you are bound to be great! Think success and act on it and you are bound to be greatly successful! Think poverty and be comfortable with it and you are bound to experience firsthand what Reinhard Bonnke meant when he said: ***"Poverty can be more dangerous than most sicknesses and diseases combined."*** Be inspired and self motivated in your thoughts because your actions and who and what you are, are the products of your thoughts! Always think positively!

Rule No. 7 >>>> Know your strengths, abilities, skills, and talents and how to use them to your employers advantages if employed. And as a rule, do not mention any weakness that has direct bearing on the progress of the prospective job.

Wisdom Keys and Action Steps:

"You are today where your thoughts have brought you. You will be tomorrow where your thoughts will take you." James Allen

"Change your thinking and your future will change." Dr. Norman Vincent Peale

"It is a great and powerful truth that, for every problem there is an answer." Abraham Lincoln

"Man's greatness lies in his power of thought." Blaise Pascal

"There are about two days which nobody should worry, and these are: yesterday and tomorrow." Robert Jones Burdett

8

Who is Your Role-model?

"If I have seen further than others it is because I stood on the shoulders of giants." **Isaac Newton**

POPULAR maxim or adage says: *"Show me your friend and I will tell you who you are."* Although this may not be the case sometimes but it does hold water. That being said, who is your role model?

Interviewers seek to know your role model by asking you the above question with a view to discovering who or the kind of person you look up to or aspire to become. Your answer will inform them whether you are a motivated and inspired applicant and your suitability for the prospective job will be brought into proper perspective. To this end therefore, having a role model in your field of specialization or endeavor will point to your interviewers that you are an inspired person dreaming to reach great heights in life or not. And having a wrong model also means having a wrong direction and vision of one's destination in view. And no employer will want to employ such an individual.

Nevertheless, the fact is that whatsoever you want to do, or whoever you want to become, a thousand and one persons have excelled in that field of endeavor and will be good mentors for you to draw inspirations from.

Am not in any way advocating imitation herein as that itself is limitation! You are the best you in existence. And you will only succeed in frustrating the real you in you should you try to be someone else other than who you are destined to be. You are a unique individual in existence.

Having said all that, it is important to have a role model who is successful or has excelled in your field of endeavor; someone you aspire to be like in future and not to imitate him or her. Moreover: **"You will make a lousy anybody else, but you are the best you in existence. You are the only you who can use your ability."** Zig Ziglar rightly observed.

And Sir Isaac Newton aptly summarized the essence of having a role model when he said: **"If I have seen further than others it is because I have stood on the shoulders of** *giants."*

Now, how do you find a role model?

Anytime you see someone you admire, someone who is getting the kind of result you would like to get, you have found a role model. A man or woman doesn't have to be perfect to be a role model. But you can draw inspiration and learn a lot from such figures.

It is in the light of this fact that you need to have a role model if hitherto you have none. That being said, it is pertinent to state here that you should watch the choice of friends keep and your role models because they speak volumes about you. And most importantly, the direction you are heading for.

My very first professional trainer in banking simply known as M.H (Mary Helen) recognized this fact when she asserted that: *"The wisdom of life consists in the elimination of the non-essentials."*

Undoubtedly, sometimes we keep friends that are not worth spending our precious time with. It was Napoleon Hill who once said that: *"You will be what you are for the next five years except for two things: the friends you keep and the kind of books you read."* And that is so true if you asked me.

Please note that it is pretty important to know some background information about your role model as job interviewers sometimes demand that you tell them something about your role model.

Rule No. 8 >>>> Have a role model and know some background information about him or her.

Wisdom Keys and Action Steps:

"Show me the man you honor, and I will know what kind of man you are, for it shows what your ideal of manhood is, what kind of man you long to be." Thomas Carlyle

"When the character of a man is not clear, look at his friends." (Japanese Proverb)

"Circumstances are the rulers of the weak, but they are the instruments of the wise." Samuel Lover

"The ultimate measure of a man is not where he stands in times of comfort and convenience but where he stands at times of challenges and controversies." Martin Luther King Jnr.

9

Job Interview Decorum

"It is your attitude, not your aptitude that will determine your altitude." John Maxwell

ATTITUDE is simply the reason why few job applicants who distinguished themselves during interview are chosen from many other applicants who passed same aptitude tests. As a matter of fact, it is possible to pass aptitude test but very easy to fail interview if you don't play the game by the rules.

In connection to the foregoing therefore, in job interview, please note that the interview begins immediately you

appear before the interview panel; and as such, your attitude positive or negative will either make or mar you during the entire exercise.

Ipso facto, it would be in your best interest to maintain a proper sense of decorum (polite and socially acceptable behavior) such as respect, politeness, courtesy, formal style of dress (corporate) and elegance.

Please permit me to sound a note of warning here that for no reason should you go into the interview hall and sit down on your own volition without been asked to do so! Some candidates have crashed out of interviews at early stage by simply and ignorantly doing so or breaking this rule as it shows lack of decorum. Be warned and informed! Courtesy demands that you should be asked to sit down before doing so and don't forget to say thank you. Imbibe a courteous and polite attitude. Note also that if you go into the interview room before trying to arrange your credentials or even without knowing your serial number as it appears on the list of successful candidates who passed aptitude test, may count against you because your orderliness and ability to organize yourself are part of the whole exercise.

Your behavior or attitude is everything you say and do. Your behavior is directly observable and the conclusions the interviewers reach about you are based on their observation of your attitude, through your experience, expectations, perceptions, thoughts, and actions. And of course, it would be in your best interest to be composed and well behaved because throughout all the stages you will be required to pass through; your attitude affects your altitude.

Rule No. 9 >>>> For no reason should you go into the interview room and sit down on your own volition without been asked to do so!

Wisdom Keys and Action Steps:

"It is your attitude, and not aptitude that will determine your altitude." John Maxwell

"If you have a dream without a problem, you don't really have a dream." John Mason

"Difficulties mastered are opportunities won." Winston Churchill

"Winning doesn't start around you, it begins inside you." Mike Murdock

"You cannot push anyone up the ladder unless he is willing to climb a little." Andrew Carnegie

10

Job Interview Dress Code

"Looking attractive in any situation is an advantage in almost any situation." Dolly kee

As an applicant going for any job interview, I know that you know that the standard and acceptable dress code is strictly formal (corporate) and do not compromise this standard for an alternative dress style if the interview is being conducted by a corporate organization.

Unfortunately, some applicants take this very important aspect of a job interview lightly by giving little or no attention to their physical appearance. Sometimes, you see such candidates dress as though they are going for a disco party or picnic. Others keep goatee and shaggy looking hair instead of clean-shaven and smart hair cut. And these careless attitudes of course, normally count against them during the exercise because your appearance speaks volumes about you.

As a criterion, your interviewers score you high or low based on your appearance; this is because it is believed that if employed, the way you dress will either project the image of the organization and profession properly or nosedive it.

Beef-up yourself image by making yourself to look fine outwardly. The way you look on the outside has a definite bearing on how you feel or see yourself in the inside. Dress up the outside.

As you are dressed, so you will be addressed. In the light of this fact therefore, dress the way you want to be addressed. Undoubtedly, every profession has its dress code and ethics; your appearance tells others a lot about what you think of yourself. Most importantly, it gives people an impression of who you are. It reveals your personality, character, sense of worth and values.

You don't have to wear expensive cloths to look good. Besides, an expensive dress does not always mean a good dress. You don't have to wear a new cloth to look neat, but you can carry yourself with poise, self respect and dignity.

It doesn't cost much to brush your teeth and rid yourself of that odor. Neither does it cost much to iron your clothes and make them look real good even if it is the only one you have.

Dress well and make sure you think well and right. Remember that the package must carry substance, that's what makes it complete. Leroy Washington said: *"When you open your mouth, you tell the world who you are."*

Dress well and think well so you can reach the next level of your life in style.

Nevertheless, don't forget that: *"Of all the things you wear, your expression is the most important."* Janet Lane reminded us. And remember that no matter how well you are dressed, you are not complete until you wear a smile and a sound mind. You are not only addressed as you are dressed but also assessed.

Rule No. 10 >>>> Dress corporate.

Wisdom Keys and Action Steps:

"As you are dressed, so you will be addressed." Anonymous

"One of the single most powerful things you can do to have influence over others is to smile at them. You are never fully dressed until you wear a smile. The best face lift is a smile." John Mason

"It is easy to dodge our responsibilities, but we cannot dodge the consequences of dodging our responsibilities." Josiah Stamp

"You are not only addressed as you are dressed but also assessed as you are dressed."

"There are no victories without conflicts, no rainbow without a cloud and storm." Aristotle

11

The Organization's Instructions

"Obedience to instructions is a high way to distinction and guarantees safe destination."

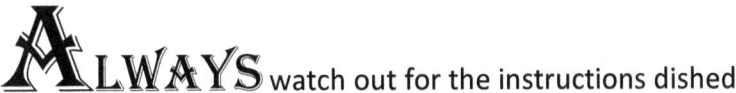 watch out for the instructions dished out by the recruiting organization you are seeking employment in take and take into cognizance the fact that it would be in your own best interest to obey them to the letter.

I have witnessed interview panel times without number

disqualified applicants who despite passing their aptitude tests failed to obey their instructions before or during interviews or because of an attempt to play smart game. Always play the game according to the rules.

Nonetheless, some of these instructions sometimes include the following among others: come with your curriculum vitae, all the original copies of your credentials and photocopies; passports, dress corporate, specified age grade and year of graduation, time of aptitude test and interview as instructed etc.

Please, kindly do yourself a favor by obeying every instruction given, otherwise, some interviewers under work pressure may simply ask you "to please take a walk." And painfully, that could end all the effort put in so afar with a view to getting the job you seek. That won't be your portion! However, to be forewarned, it has been said, is to be forearmed.

Note that intelligence and aptitude tests are normally conducted with a view to discovering your IQ (Intelligence quotient), whereas, job interview is conducted to discover your attitude, capability and suitability for the prospective job. Interestingly, it is the combination of your aptitude and attitude that your employers take into consideration before giving you the job. And remember that obedience is better than sacrifice. And as John Maxwell would say, it is your attitude and not aptitude that will determine your altitude.

Rule No. 11 >>>> Obey the organization's instructions to the letter.

Wisdom Keys and Action Steps:

"Obedience is better than sacrifice." (The Bible)

"Make a list of everything that is holding you back. Then handle each task or issue one at a time until you are free." Brain Koslow

"Men's nature are alike, it is their habits that carry them far apart." Confucius

"The men who build the future are those who know that greater things are yet to come, and that they themselves will help bring them about."

"Fear not tomorrow, God is already there." E. C. McKenzie

12

Manage Your Time

"The man who dares to waste one hour of his time has not discovered the value of life." Charles Darwin

"There is never enough time to do everything, but there is always enough time to do the most important things." Law of forced efficiency by Brian Tracy

BANKS and so many other reputable and time conscious organizations no doubt, follow Charles Darwin's principle and the Brian Tracy's law of forced efficiency of time management to the letter.

As an applicant, you must learn to manage your time

effectively; be punctual and always on time.

You have no justifiable excuse(s) not to be at work and get the job done when it should be done as a bank staff; rain, long distance, or hold up notwithstanding, you just have to manage your time and find your way to the office at stipulated time by the management or get ready to "dance to the music" should you do otherwise.

So also, as an applicant going for a job interview, endeavor not to be late or you may be disqualified.

All of us are graciously and equally endowed with 24 hours daily courtesy time and nature, but the difference however, is that great people make every seconds, minutes and hours of their time count but: *"Those who make worst use of their time complain of its shortness*." Orisonswett Marden observed.

It was Benjamin Franklin who said that: *"He who is good at making excuses is seldom good for anything else."* And George Washington Carver wasn't wrong when he declared that: *"Ninety-nine percent of failures come from people who have the habit of making excuses."*

Against this backdrop therefore, it is high time you stopped giving excuses or complaining about limitation of time factor, instead, plan and spend your time wisely you would spend your money. And remember that wasted time cannot be regained. Every seconds, minutes and hours we lose can never be rewinded. It is true that time if properly viewed, is better than money. Yes, you can get more money, you cannot get more time.

Rule No. 12 >>>> Manage you time efficiently and never be late for a job interview.

Wisdom Keys and Action Steps:

"Tell me how you use your time and money, and I will tell you where and what you will be ten years from now." Napoleon Hill

"The man who dares to waste one hour of his time has not discovered the value of life." Charles Darwin

"Time is more valuable than money. You can get more money but you can't get more time." Jim Rohn

"If I could I would stand on a busy corner, hat in hand and beg people to throw me their wasted hours." Bernard Berenson

"Those who make worst use of their time complain of its shortness." Orisonswett Marden

"He who masters his time masters his life." Mike Murdock

"Your success or failure depends on how you use your time. Time is moving on...are you?" Willie Jolley

"Hard work means prosperity; only fools idle away their time." (Proverbs 12:11 NLT)

"If you take care of the minutes in your life, hours will take care of themselves." Lord Chesterfield

"We always have enough time, if we will but use it aright." John Wolfgang

"There is never enough time to do everything, but there is always enough time to do the most important things." Brian Tracy (Law of forced efficiency)

"To be successful in the transactions and investments of life, you must be time conscious." Dr. Paul Enenche

13

Watch Your Grammar & Body Language

What did you read? The interviewer may ask.

PLEASE note that your grammatical expressions and body language which are both obvious and very conspicuous can either make or mar your job interview if not properly handled or taken care of. Against this backdrop therefore, it is quite pertinent to exercise the above frequently asked question by job interviewers to ascertain whether you are grammatically sound.

Job Interviewer: What did you read?

You (Applicant): I read (/red/pp) or studied... let's say Law for instance.

Now, note the usage of past participle in answering the above question in lieu of present tense. As such, it is of utmost importance to know the usages of tenses and concord rules.

But wait a moment; am I trying to teach you English Language rules or something you already know? Smiles... No please, but to stress the need for speaking simple and correct English Language instead of high sounding grammar and vocabularies during job interview.

Of course, some candidates are normally rated low in this aspect of job interview criterion. So, it would be in your own interest to know tenses and their usages very well.

As a matter of fact, owing to a wrong body language, an applicant was once disqualified and asked to take a walk out of the interview room because he went in, without been asked to, he sat down on his own volition and permission, (not confidently but arrogantly) even before he was asked to sit down; and as if that blunder was not enough, he crossed his legs and putting on airs of importance and waiting for the interviewers to greet him. Guess what happened! Of course, he was shown the way to the exit door. Always remember that: "It is your attitude, and not aptitude that will determine your altitude." John Maxwell cautioned.

Yes, the applicant passed the **aptitude** test quite aright but failed the **attitude** test woefully.

At this juncture, let's examine some standard, appropriate and internationally acceptable body language to maintain or observe during job interview:

- Maintain eye contact and face the interviewers.
- Your facial expression should be warm, friendly, and relaxed; smile if necessary.
- Nod your head to indicate concurrence and interest while listening to what your interviewers are saying.
- Open your arms, don't fold them.
- Use open-palmed gestures, if you are the type that gesticulates while speaking. Do not clench your fists or tap your fingers.
- Sit back but do not relax backwards on your chair.
- Do not sit with both legs crossed.
- When appropriate, offer handshakes with genuine warmth and interest. And please, do not initiate a handshake with your interviewer except if he or she extends his or her hand first.
- Do not frown, instead SMILE, smile can disarm anybody; your interviewers inclusive.

Rule No. 13 >>>> Speak simple and correct formal English Language. Avoid informal expressions or slangs; maintain good eye contact and body language.

Wisdom Keys and Action Steps:

"Never outgrow manners and decorum no matter your status and achievement."

"The people who get on in this life are people who get up and look for the circumstances they want, and if they can't find them, make them." George Bernard Shaw

"In this life we can only get those things for which we hunt, for which we strive and for which we are willing to make sacrifice." George Adams

"A small man stands on others. A great man stands on God." John Mason

"The reason why you are bordering on so many things is because you have not decided one." John Mason

"A wise man will make more opportunity than he finds." Francis Bacon

"If you dare for nothing, you need hope for nothing." John Mason

"Never, never, never, never, never give up!" Winston Churchill

14

The Place of Experience

"What do you think you have to offer us that we do not have or other applicants do not have?" The Interviewer

U NDOUBTEDLY, job interviewers sometimes ask the above or similar question with a view to discovering your uniqueness, potentials or talents, practical skills, knowledge and experience that you can bring on board and to bear on the prospective job if employed.

It is "vital essential" to bear this fact in mind while answering such a tricky question during job interview.

A female applicant was once asked the above tricky question by a job interview panel; unfortunately and ignorantly, she replied: "I have a Higher Diploma." The interviewer insisted she wasn't the only Higher Diploma holder attending the interview and she said: "*I am a woman.*" And guess what! She was disqualified! Such answer clearly shows that despite that fact that she was a graduate and did pass the aptitude test, she was ignorant in the art of interview and was not prepared for the exercise. Of course, interviewers don't waste their precious time on such applicants but normally move on in search of candidates who know their onion and trust me; they know and can easily identify applicants who are prepared.

Experience is a very important factor in some jobs and a criterion job employers look out for in candidates.

More so, you may rightly subscribe to the school of thought which holds that no knowledge gained is waste and that experience (i.e. the process of gaining knowledge or skill over a period of time through seeing and doing things rather than through studying) is the best teacher.

Against this backdrop therefore, it would be in your interest to include in your Cv. Past working experiences if you have any and you are sure you can defend your claims if asked questions based on them.

Nowadays, you need experience to get a job but without job

you cannot get experience- it is a vicious circle no doubt. But not to worry because with God, your attitude and the stuff you are made of that will distinguish you and guarantee you a place in the job market.

Rule No. 14 >>>> Express your willingness to bring your past relevant experience to bear on the job if employed.

Wisdom Keys and Action Steps:

"If you stop learning, you will start dying." Benson Idahosa

"Learning has bitter roots but bears sweet fruits" Anonymous

"You will remain the same person you are for the next five years, except for two things: the books you read and the friends you keep." Napoleon Hill

"Every situation properly viewed is an opportunity." John Mason

"Few things in the world are more powerful than a positive push. A smile; a word of optimism and hope; a "you can do it" when things are tough." Richard De Vas

"You will never see the sun rise by looking to the west. Opportunities can drop in your laps if you have your lap where opportunities drop." John Mason

15

Job Interview Dos and Don'ts

Do the "dos" and don't the "don'ts".

JOB interview has a lot of unwritten rules and regulations that should be taken into cognizance as an applicant. And to pass the exercise with all smiles, here are some "dos" and "don'ts" to observe among others:

Maintain formal or Standard English language throughout the exercise and avoid the usages of slangs and colloquial expressions. Yes, an applicant once walked into an interview room frowning and when asked why he was frowning at the interviewers, he said: ***"I am damned stressed up."*** And the interviewer who was "shocked" and "perplexed" by his response curiously asked: ***"What did you just say?"*** And on realizing that he has goofed by using inappropriate language, he apologized thus: ***"Sorry it was a slip of the tongue."*** And believe it or not, but that was how he got himself slipped out of the job interview process.

>Please learn to smile always. It doesn't cost anything to smile yet it has a tremendous positive impact on both the giver and receiver. And note that your interviewers prefer to see you smiling to frowning.
>
>Dress decently and be well groomed.
>
>Avoid complaining, excuses, and introduction of negative impression during the interview.
>
>Do not lie because you will only succeed in disqualifying yourself. Having said that, there may be certain details about you that I know that you know are better left unsaid during job interview. And remember that the interview room is not a confessional; and you are not going therein to confess your sins to a priest or are you? (Smiles...)
>
>Do not sit down with your legs crossed.
>
>Never be late for job interviews.
>Have with you at least three (3) copies of your C.V. or more and originals and photocopies of all your relevant credentials and recent passport photographs orderly arranged before the exercise proper. Note that trying to

sort out or arrange your credentials during the exercise may score you low in composure and orderliness.

Do not frown at the interviewers for whatsoever reason. An experienced interviewer may sometimes tease you to see your reaction and how you may handle their clients in similar situation.

Do not interrupt or argue with the interviewers because by doing so, you will only succeed in disqualifying yourself.

Obey their instructions to the letter.

"Do not smoke even if the interviewer lights up cigarette and encourages you to do likewise." Ron Fry.

Say "Please excuse me" if you belch or cough.

Sure you have got a nice phone; but kindly switch off your phone throughout the exercise.

Be enthusiastic throughout the interview process.

Do not exaggerate your abilities, experience, accomplishment and responsibilities. Lying about these, can have a negative effect on your interview.

Do not be condescending, shaming, temperamental, judgmental, impolite, critical, harsh, and angry or exhibit any anti-social behavior.

Be yourself. Do not sound like any other person. Be positive, courteous, thoughtful, enthusiastic and friendly.

Do not introduce any negative impression throughout your interaction with the interviewers; and do not argue or interrupt the interviewers! (This is the Golden Rule of job interview!)

Rule No. 15 >>>> Simply do the "dos" and don't the "don'ts".

Wisdom Keys and Action Steps:

"The wisdom of life consists in the elimination of the non-essentials." M. H

"In the end, the people who fail are those who never try." David Viscot

"A man is not finished when he is defeated, he is finished when he quits." Richard Nixon

"Beware of little expenses. A little leak can sink a great ship." Anonymous

"What hurts, instructs." Anonymous

"Success begins the moment we understand that life is about beginning." John Mason

"How we manage our pain is a major factor in learning to manage life." Mick Brooks

"What doesn't destroy me makes me stronger." Martin Luther King

"Another attitude to adopt if you are to ride the winds of adversity is this- focus on the fact that some of the greatest lessons and advances we make in life are those which come out of suffering." Selwyn Hughes

"I have been through the best university the world can offer- the University of Adversity." John Major

16

Job Interview Pitfalls to be Avoided

"If the frog in front falls in a pit, others behind take caution." African Proverb

One of the pitfalls to be avoided is the falsification of credentials.

An applicant once attended a bank job interview; performed creditably well in the aptitude test but succeeded in getting herself disqualified from the exercise as a consequence of falsification of her age on her statement of result despite the stern warning stipulating that: *"Any alteration or erasure renders this document invalid and valueless."*

Other desperate applicants, owing to far reaching conditions normally stipulated or spelt out by employers of labor, falsify educational results. Some others give what can best be described as a "soccer age" as their age and unfortunately end up exposing themselves during interview. Abraham Lincoln once said: *"No man has enough good memory to make a successful liar."* ((Smiles...)

The job interviewers are no kids or fools. They are highly intelligent and experienced sets of individuals and could easily detect when you tell them lies. Ipso facto therefore, **honesty still remains the best policy to adopt.**

It would do you some good to recognize the fact that job interview is not a do or die affairs; and as such, if you are not there yet, at least you are somewhere. And better still, you can harness your God given potentials, be self employed and possibly live far better than some of us with the so called white collar jobs. That's so true!

Have you ever thought about it, observed or noticed that most people who are doing exceptionally well and have got themselves fame, power and riches to be reckoned with all over the world and in all walks of life are either exploiting their naturally endowed potentials or are self employed and not working for some employers? Hear this and hear me well, you can quote me if you like: *no job or employer, I repeat, no job or employer will ever and can ever pay you better than what your talents/potentials will pay you if properly harnessed!* Think about it! So why do the unimaginable with a view to getting a job? Always be positive minded and optimistic for there is a hope even for a tree that has been cut down let alone you.

Rule No. 16 >>>> Never falsify credentials or give claims you cannot defend.

Wisdom Keys and Action Steps:

"Dare to dream and act on that dream. The Acts of Apostles was written because the Apostles acted." **John Maxwell**

"The secret of getting things done is to do it now." **Napoleon Hill**

"Think ahead, plan ahead, work ahead and you will get ahead in life." **Dr Paul Enenche**

"Prayer moves the hand that moves the world." **David Watson**

"Problems are only opportunities in working clothes." **Henry J. Kaiser**

"Challenges are not in any way signs that you cannot make it, but proof that there is something better at the end of the tunnel if you don't give up. Remember, life without problems is an illusion."

17

Job Interview Etiquettes

Use your knowledge of etiquettes to distinguish yourself from the crowd.

Why etiquette in job interview? It is very essential because many applicants crash out of the highly competitive job interviews owing to unintentional breach of manners; and for those who desire to distinguish themselves from the crowd with uniqueness and by going extra mile and to be given a place in the highly competitive job market wherein there are fewer openings with thousands of applicants competing.

It was Zig Ziglar who said: *"**Desire is the "extra" that makes the little difference and it's the little difference that makes the big difference in life.**"*

Most times there are few available job vacancies but with thousands of applicants usually in attendance and as a matter of fact, have got the requisite qualifications for the job; as such, you need to distinguish yourself out of the crowd in order to be given a place, and of course, you need a pretty good knowledge of etiquette to do just that.

Etiquette other than its literal meaning (i.e. formal standard of rules of correct and polite behavior in society or among members of a profession), according to Stern & Kay include:

*Presenting yourself with polish that shows you can be taken seriously.

*It is being comfortable around people.

*It is making people comfortable around you.

*It is being courteous and behaving appropriately.

*Etiquette helps minimize mistakes.

Basic Rule:

*Be thoughtful and courteous to people (your interviewers inclusive), smile.

*Be appreciative-say "thank you" when appropriate.

*Don't raise your voice-lowering it might get you more attention (but be audible).

Rule No. 17 >>>> Use your knowledge of etiquette to distinguish yourself from the crowd.

Wisdom Keys and Action Steps:

"To finish the race, stay on the track." **John Maxwell**

"Haste will only cause you waste." **Anonymous**

"The greatest assassin of dream is haste, and the desire to reach things before the right time." **John Mason**

"You can change everything for better if you change yourself for better." **Anonymous**

"There are two quick ways to disaster: taking nobody's advice and taking everybody's advice." **John Mason**

"Winning is not everything but the effort to win is." **Zig Ziglar**

"It is difficulties which show what men are." **Epictetus**

"Gold is tried by fire, brave men by adversity." **Seneca**

"Find out what you are good at, and work on those skills, they are the raw materials from which you shape your destiny." Bill Newman

18

Never Fear the Interviewers

"Fear is a magnet that moves you in direction opposite your desire. And the cure to fear is to do that which you fear to do." Abraham Lincoln

PLEASE, it would be in your own interest not to enter the interview room in fear and trembling because your body language will sell you off to your interviewers who just like you, are also part of the human species or human beings with flesh and blood and not some fearful monsters. (Smiles..)

There is no gain denying the fact that some interviewers can be harsh, aggressive and sometimes, intimidating; while others can be friendly. But you need not fear them. Just be cautious and courteous and behave yourself.

Fear is not positive at all and never has it been a God given spirit! And as such, fear should be rejected by faith anytime it springs up or rear its ugly head. Remember: *"For God has not given you the spirit of fear, but of love, boldness and a sound mind."*

John Maxwell explained fear using business terminologies thus: *"Fear is interest paid on a debt you may never owe."* So, why fear your interviewers?

Eleanor Roosevelt provided us with an effective and practical antidote to fear when he said: *"I believe that one can conquer fear by doing the things he fears to do."*

Do not fear your interviewers but respect them. See them as you would see your friends and be comfortable and feel at ease with them.

Rule No. 18 >>>> Do not fear the interviewers but respect them. And as a rule, DO NOT argue or interrupt them if they are talking; let them finish before you talk. Otherwise, you will only succeed in disqualifying yourself from the exercise.

Wisdom Keys and Action Steps:

"The greatest mistake you can make in life is to continually fear that you will make one." **John Mason**

"Until you violently move against your fears, your life will not experience a change." **Dr Paul Enenche**

"No man can make you feel inferior without your consent." **Eleanor Roosevelt**

"Fear and failure are as connected as the sun and the shadow or the snail and the shell." **Dr Paul Enenche**

"Fear is interest paid on a debt you may not owe." **John Maxwell**

"Don't be afraid to fail. Don't waste energy trying to cover up failure. If you are not failing, you are not growing." **Anonymous**

"When we challenge our fears, we master them. When we wrestle with our problems, they lose their grip on us. When we dare to confront the things that scare us, we open the door to personal liberty." **Anonymous**

19

Face to Face with the Interviewers

You only have first time to make first impression.

ALWAYS remember that first impression matters a lot and that you only have first time to make first impression.

To this end therefore, permit me to reiterate that: the moment you enter the interview room and come face to face with your interviewers, note that the interview has already started. This is because they begin to observe your dress code, personal appearance and cleanliness, body language, and facial expression the moment you step into the interview room; and it would be in your interest to greet them appropriately with smile and observe social decorum and **for no reason should you sit down on your volition until you are asked to do so!**

Otherwise, it amounts to faux pas (i.e. an action which causes embarrassment because it is not socially correct) and some harsh interviewers may be angry at you and even ask you to "take a walk" out of the office or pose this question to you: "Who asked you to sit down!?" And starting a job interview on that note can have a negative consequence on you and worst of all, dim your chances of getting the job you seek.

Be informed. And remember that you only have first time to make first impression.

Nevertheless, do not frown at them no matter what as it would create a wrong impression about you. Instead SMILE, and that is the expression they prefer to see you wear.

Carlo Ancelotti as a soccer coach had once experienced a poor starting in his coaching career and realized the importance of first impression by starting well and aptly cautioned that: *"If you start your career poorly, you never get another chance."* Carle Barde advised that: *"Though no one can go back and make a brand new start, anyone can start from now and make a brand new beginning."*

Undoubtedly, you cannot correct the past but you can

correct the future by not repeating same mistakes of the past. And probably you might have attended job interview in the past and made some mistakes and faux pas ignorantly, there is absolutely nothing you can do about the past; but the good news is that when next you go for another interview, be sure you can do better because now, you know better.

Mike Murdock was most definitely right when he said: **"Don't poison your future with the pains of the past. Stop looking at where you have been and start looking at where you can be."**

Rule No. 19 >>>> You have only first time to make first impression. Do not frown at your interviewers but always smile (though not unnecessarily) and behave well.

Wisdom Keys and Action Steps:

"Do not fake things in order to impress others. Be your natural self."

"Remember there are two benefits of failure. First, if you do fail, you learn what doesn't work; and second, the failure gives you an opportunity to try a new approach. Most people think of failure and success as two opposites, but they are actually both products of the same process." Roger Von Oech

"Where there is danger, there lurks opportunity. Where there is opportunity, there lurks danger. The two go together." Earle Nightingale

"The door of opportunity won't open until you push. Don't sit back and take what comes. Go after what you want." John Mason

"Procrastination is the grave in which opportunity is buried." John Mason

20

The Job interview (Sample Questions & Answering Guides)

"When you open your mouth, you tell the world who you truly are." Leroy Washington

Now, we have come to the crux of the matter.

Take into cognizance the fact that you will be examined by the interviewers to know who you are, your attitude, skills, abilities and experiences among others. And all these, they will be able to ascertain through your responses to their questions.

Try visualizing and imagining yourself sitting face to face with your job interviewers and they have copies of your C.V. then the exercise begins proper.

* **Interviewer:** Now, tell me about yourself.

You: My name is Three16. (Not my names are ... even when you have up to five names). The above question is **unavoidable in any job interview** and can be asked in several ways. And that is a golden opportunity for you to express and sell yourself to the interviewers by talking about your educational background, skills, knowledge, talents, experience with relevance to the prospective job. *(Apply rule no. 7 and don't forget rule no. 4 then summarize and be brief as possible)*

***Interviewer:** Is that all?

You: Yes please. (Wear a smile as it would help to diffuse tension while expecting and listening to the next question; nod where necessary and be sure you understand the next question before answering lest you "misfire")

***Interviewer:** How old are you?

You: Of course, you know your age. **(Remember rule no. 16 and be warned!)**

***Interviewer:** Are you married?

You: Yes please. Or no please. (**Answer as it applies to you**

and in case your interviewer is worried or thinks your marital status will affect your work, convince him or her that you do not take family affairs to work.)

*Interviewer: What did you read?

You: (Apply rule no.15 in answering such type of question). I read Mass Communication and law; for instance.

*Interviewer: How would explain Mass Communication (i.e. the course you studied) to a lay man?

You: (Apply rule no.15 again). And remember, the course you studied may not be relevant to the job you are being interviewed for. But not to worry, that is not their concern; they want to know if you can express yourself or better still, fit into the job on offer.

*Interviewer: Why do you want to work with us?

You: (Apply rule no. 2). This is the reason why you are there in the first place. You want to work therein to earn a living and shoulder your responsibilities. Isn't? 9Smiles...) I guess that's why you need a job. (**And please avoid using applicant's platitude as in: "I want to contribute my quota to the organization and all that."**)

*Interviewer: Why us and not others in your field?

You: (application of rule no. 4 &2 will come in handy). And they will be impressed to know that you have done your home work well about their organization and treat you as a serious candidate.

Besides, you probably want to work with them because of their conducive working atmosphere, prestige and no doubt, their nice and attractive welfare package. (Smiles...)

*Interviewer: I see; so what is it that you have to offer us that you think we do not have or that other candidates do not have?

You: Note that the more you answer their questions, the tougher it becomes. (**Apply rule no.16 in answering such type of tricky question**) I believe there is always room for improvement. So, if employed, I will always think of better and creative ways of doing and improving my job by bringing my talent, skills, abilities and experience to bear on the job positively.

*Interviewer: Now tell me, what is it that you don't like about yourself?

You: (watch out! This is dangerous!) **Remember the golden rule and do not mention anything negative that can disrupt the progress of the prospective job. And in case you must mention a weakness, explain what you have done about it. As in:** I am slow in typing but I am taking a course to improve my typing skills and speed. **Note that you have not only succeeded in stylishly dodging that bomb, but indirectly let you interviewer know that you are computer literate; a knowledge which of course, most employers desire their employees possess. Always think fast don't be in a hurry to answer such type of question.**

Note that you must not mention any flaw that may hamper

the progress of the job! And should they insist that you mention one, it should be a weakness that you have already corrected and may have no direct bearing on the prospective job.

*Interviewer: How well can you cope with stress or can you really work under pressure?

You: Of course, you will always rise up to challenges and adapt easily to any working condition you find yourself. Or don't you think so? (Smiles) Your response shouldn't be far from that direction.

*Interviewer: Who is your role model?

You: (This is exactly where you need rule no. 8) Three16 for example. (Smiles….)

*Interviewer: Why the choice of Three16? And tell me something about him.

You: (Again, rule no. 8 will come in handy)

*Interviewer: What is the name of your state governor?

You: (Note that any current affairs questions on recent happenings may be asked and as such, the habit and application of rule no. 5 will help out here.)

*Interviewer: Where did you work before now and why did you leave there?

You: (You know better and the application of rule no. 16 will be most definitely right)

*Interviewer: Do your skills match this job? Or why do you think you will succeed on this job?

You: (Apply rules no. 4 & 16 while answering the question). Sure, your skills match the job and even if they don't, express your willingness to acquire the needed skills if given the opportunity. And of course, you will succeed on the job because you have the right mindset.

*Interviewer: What makes you angry?

You: Injustice. (**You know better. But always remember the job interview golden rule**)

*Interviewer: How do you react if you are angry?

You: (Caution! Remember the golden rule!) You think before reacting bearing in mind the consequences of irrational reaction of anger. And always try to put your temper under control be keeping calm. Isn't it? (Smiles...)

*Interviewer: You are sharp and we will like to give you the job. Now tell us, how do you balance life and work?

You: (Apply rules no.4 & 12). Thank you. And I guess you think everything in life is regulated by time and there is time for everything. It's all about being organized and your ability to manage your time effectively. I work when it is time for work. I hope you understand.

*Interviewer: Do you take work home with you?

You: (Apply rule no. 12). The interviewer wants know if you are a procrastinator! As such, your response should be in this wise: there is the need to beat deadline and get work done when it should be done within the time frame for the work.

*Interviewer: Which good book have you read lately or recently?

You: (Application of rule no.3 will be useful here.)

*Interviewer: If given the opportunity, would you like to go to school to improve your qualification?

You: Yes please. (Or would you have said no? Smiles...)

*Interviewer: Where would you like to work?

You: (You know better than I do.)

*Interviewer: What if your employer decides otherwise, would you still work?

You: Yes please.

*Interviewer: How much would you like to earn as a monthly salary?

You: (Remember rule no.19 and the application of rule no.2 will guide you herein as you would have known what the take home pay is like for candidates of your level and do not demand above it. If they insist you mention the amount you want; be diplomatic as in: I want my salary to commensurate with my work.)

*Interviewer: What will you do with your first salary?

You: (Remember rule no.4 and be sensible in your

response)

*Interviewer: Thank you for coming. We will get back to you.

You: Thank you and do have a nice day.

Note that your response to their questions will certainly attract more questions but not to worry, just remember rule no 13 & 17 as the whole interview is just questions and answers exercise.

And by the time you have answered the above or similar questions and several others; the interviewers will have discovered who you are, your attitude, confidence, experience, enthusiasm, versatility, dependability, etc. and whether you are likely or suitable for the job. And of course, you are, having known these guides at your finger tips and with God on your side, success is in view.

Rule No. 20 >>>>. The golden rule is never introduce any negative impression throughout your interaction with the interviewers.

Wisdom Keys and Action Steps:

"Success does not happen by mere wish; it is made to happen. Stop wishing things to happen and start making them happen." David Oyedepo

"I like things to happen, if they don't happen, I like to make them happen." John Mason

"Do not wait until you are perfect before you are productive." E. A. Adeboye

"If you can't fly, run. If you can't run, walk. If you can't walk, crawl. By all means, keep moving forward. " Martin Luther King jnr

"Heroes are people who do what has to be done regardless of the consequences." Anonymous

"Restlessness is discontent and discontent is the first necessity of progress. Show me a thoroughly satisfied man and I will show you a failure." Thomas Edison

"The realities of your own life tomorrow are already in the pictures that dominate your imagination today." Sam Adeyemi

"One sound idea is all that one needs to achieve success." Napoleon Hill

"Winners don't win because they do different things; they win because they do same things differently." Anonymous

21

Job interview General Questions & Answering Guides

NORMALLY, some questions asked during job interview are based on your CV. or resume and others on past experience etc. So, don't forget to include in your CV. Past trainings or experiences you have got that are relevant to the prospective job. In the same vein, do not include any claim you cannot convincingly defend as by so doing may sell you out to your interviewers.

Interestingly, a few other questions that may be thoughts provoking, current affairs based, funny, puzzling, rational, and sometimes "irrational" are asked with a view to involving or engaging you in a dialogue and of course, to find out whether you are suitable for the job and to know how vastly experienced you are.

You cannot, I repeat, you cannot escape similar or some of the questions herein; as such, be encouraged to familiarize yourself with how best to answer them in your own words if need be.

However, the list of such questions is inexhaustible and the truth is this: expect the unexpected; and please note that you must not answer all the questions that may be thrown at you correctly before being given the job provided you are found suitable for the job and avoid introducing negative impressions throughout your interaction with the interviewers. Shun unnecessary explanations while the interview lasts. Be brief and concise.

Now, pay rapt attention to questions wherein you see "caution" because your response to such "tricky" questions can either make or mar your chances of getting the job. ***And endeavor to think and articulate your responses to match the needs and benefits of your employer because that is exactly what your interviewers want to hear.***

Below are likely job interview general questions you may encounter and answering guides:

28. **Interviewer: Tell us about yourself.**

You: (By now, I guess you know what to do. Isn't it?) Market yourself.

29. **Interviewer: What are your assets or strengths?**

You: Probably you are versatile; quick to learn, have the ability to work under pressure and deliver results within reasonable time, a team player etc. just go ahead and tell them your strengths or skills that are relevant to the job.

30. **Interviewer: What are your goals five years from now?**

Caution!

You: Do not give the impression that you want to work briefly with them and leave for a better job or school even if that is your intention. Instead, try to align your goals with your employer's in that you hope to have acquired more experiences on the job, and based on your performance, get promoted or more responsibilities and possibly, improved welfare packages.

31. **Interviewer: Who has inspired you in life and why?**

You: Note that this is another way of asking who is your role model and why? (**Apply rule no.8**)

32. **Interviewer: How well do you spend your time or how well do you manage your time?**

You: (Application of rule no.12 will be quite relevant)

33. **Interviewer: Are you a team player?**

You: Of course, you are; because you find it easy to work and get along easily with others.

34. **Interviewer: What experience do you have in this field?**

Or are you experienced?

You: (Application of rule no.16 will be the right thing to do if you are an experienced candidate). **And just in case you lack experience in the field, admit it and express your willingness to learn and improve on the job if given the opportunity.**

35. Interviewer: What irritates you about a co-worker? Or tell me about the best or worst boss you have worked with. Or what type of people do you have trouble getting along with?

Caution!

You: If you answer such or similar questions negatively by ignorantly mentioning their weaknesses, you need no prophet to tell you that you are not far from the exit door. **This is because your interviewers may rightly or wrongly think that you have attitude problem and will say the same thing about them to other and worst still, may not be able to get along with your employers, other workers who behave differently from you or their or clients or the public. And be informed that it is very possible that the person interviewing you may be one of the superiors you may be working closely with if employed. So be guided.**

By that very fact therefore, in answering such tricky question, always remember the golden rule. You recognize the fact that there are individual differences and human beings are not perfect, so you always try to be tolerant and this has been helping you to get along with people irrespective of their behaviors. **Or don't you think so?**

36. Interviewer: Do you prefer to work alone or with others?

Caution!

You: You must have boasted of being a team player earlier on or in your CV. And admitting now that you prefer to work alone will send a wrong signal to your interviewers. **Be consistent in your response.**

37. Interviewer: How do you handle change?

You: It would be in your interest to admit that you handle change well. Show that you can accept and adapt to changes at work or in business easily. And in case you have a positive change experience in the past, go ahead and say so.

38: Interviewer: What do you know about our organization?

You: (This is exactly where rule no.2 will help you out. Answering nothing will send a wrong signal meaning that you are not prepared for the interview or interested in the organization)

39. Interviewer: Are you willing to travel outside the state, work overtime, night or weekends?

Caution!

You: It would be in your own interest not to disagree at this point in time. Besides, rule no.2 should have told you that about the organization earlier enough.

40. Interviewer: What have you heard about our organization that you didn't like?

Caution!

You: That's a land mine! And I guess you still remember the golden rule. Ok, this is the way out: (Apply rule no.2) and probably you must have heard that the organization lay off staff months ago and may be that is why there is vacancy, or they declared loss etc. positively express your wish that the organization will improve in that regard. Or better still; ask them what the organization is doing to cushion that effect? It is not wrong to do so.

41. Interviewer: What do you like to do when you are not at work?

You: Note that this is another way of asking what is your hobby? **It would be wise to talk about activities that contribute positively to you as a person and to your job.**

42. Interviewer: How do you balance your work and family life?

You: (Apply rule no.12): You are an organized person who put things where they belong and as such do not allow family or personal affairs interfere with your work. Am I right? (Smiles...) Answer in that direction.

43. Interviewer: Tell me honestly about the strong and weak points of your boss, your company and management team.

Caution!

You: Again that's a land mine! And if you are not careful in answering that kind of tricky and implicating question, you are strictly on your own. **Remember you are not in a confessional to confess your "sins" to some "saints" and apply the golden rule.**

44. Interviewer: In September 11 th, 2001; there was a terrorist attack on World Trade Centre. Who masterminded the attack?

You: Note that questions on any current issues may be asked. **And if you didn't ignore rule no.5, you will find it handy in such situation.**

45. Interviewer: Why do you think you will do well on this job?

You: You have just been issued a blank cheque or rather, given a life line! Whether the job you are being interviewed for is in your field of study or not, provided you have passed the aptitude test and possess the requisite skills or experience, this is a golden opportunity to say what stuff you are made up of with relevance to the job.

46. Interviewer: Why should I hire you? Or what do you have to offer that others don't have? Or what is special about you?

You: If asked any of the above or similar question, do as in above.

47. Interviewer: May I contact your referee or present employer for a reference?

Caution!

You: Note that outright refusal will surely send a wrong signal. This is how to handle such dagger whenever it is thrown at you: **(Watch your body language and apply rule no.4)** If your current employer or referee is aware that you are attending the interview, why not? But if not, be diplomatic and express they wish that you prefer they hear about the interview from you first before they contact them. And of course, expect a follow up question from an experienced interviewer.

48. Interviewer: So tell me, which excuse did you give your employer or supervisor before coming for this interview?

Caution!

You: If you mistakenly or ignorantly give the negative impression that you lied or feigned you were sick. Then, if you are not out yet, you are just an inch away from the interview room as the interviewer may just end the session with "Thanks for coming. We will contact you." And I guess you know what that means! **Stay on track therefore, always remember the golden rule. So, probably you were on break, casual leave or off duty etc. you know better.**

49. Interviewer: What have you been doing since you left school or your last job?

Caution!

You: You wouldn't give the impression that you have been lazing around or idling away your time or would you?

50. Interviewer: Tell me about a time you helped a colleague at work.

You: You claimed you are a team player. Isn't? Probably your colleague was once sick or on annual leave without a reliever and you had to cover for him or her without additional pay or incentive whatsoever.

51. Interviewer: How do you get along with old co-workers?

You: Hope you would respect them; establish rapport with them, be willing to learn from their experiences and have a cordial working relationship with them. Or don't you think so?

52. Interviewer: What do co workers, family members or friends say about you?

You: (Apply rule no.4). You know your strengths and so just go ahead and put them in their mouths.

53. Interviewer: What is more important to you: money or the work?

Caution!

You: Both are important but work is more important because you need work to get money. Isn't?

54. Interviewer: If you won $10 million lottery, would you still work?

You: I just hope you would still work and of course, make the money work for you. Besides, what if you never won the lottery in the first place, wouldn't you work?

55. Interviewer: What would you say to your boss if he is crazy about an idea you think is dead wrong?

Caution!

You: Note that outright refusal to accept the idea or instruction of your boss amounts to gross insubordination and the attendant consequences! So I thought you would be diplomatic enough to **accept your boss's idea/instruction and respectfully present your position or take on the matter and if he insists, then you just have to do it your boss's way provided it is within the confines of the policies of the organization.** Your response shouldn't be far from that.

56. Interviewer: Describe your management style.

You: Given the opportunity, I guess you would be a manager or a leader who believes in working together with others to achieve set goals and objectives, and as such, teach, delegate and share responsibilities and works fairly among your workers.

57. Interviewer: Have you ever worked with someone you didn't like?

Caution!

You: (Apply the golden rule). You try to be tolerant as much as you can and as well judge people based on their performance and work and not on their behavior towards you. And that makes it easier for you to get along with others.

58. Interviewer: Are you computer literate?

You: (Rule no.6 will come very handy)

59. Interviewer: What was the toughest part of your last job?

You: You know better. And as a rule, do not introduce any negative impression.

60. Interviewer: Do you consider yourself successful?

You: I hope you do. Give both personal and job related examples of what success means to you and let them reflect your employer's goals. As in: You consider yourself successful because you have dreams and visions and set goals; and you have achieved some of your targets and on track towards achieving others.

61. Interviewer: What does failure mean to you? Have you ever failed before?

You: The interviewer wants to know if you are honest. You may give a past experience of a setback you had and the positive lesson you learnt thereof. And remember to shun negativity!

62. Interviewer: What do you worry about?

Caution!

You: Answering such question headlong may reveal an earlier concealed weakness. As such, I wish there are two things you don't worry about: yester and tomorrow; the things you can change and the things you cannot change.

63. Interviewer: Why are you applying for a job other than your field of specialization?

You: If you are like me who read Mass Communication and Law for example, but working professionally as a banker. Then you may be asked this kind of question. But not to worry, as long as you passed the aptitude test, you have got the interviewer's attention and if employed, you will be trained off and on the job. (**Apply rule no. 4**) Talk about the relevance of your area of specialization, experience, or skills that you can bring to bear on the prospective job.

64. Interviewer: Have you ever been convicted? Or have you ever been arrested?

Caution!

You: (Please be informed that the interviewers are not entitled to invade your privacy!). **And if you forget the golden rule in situation like this, you are strictly on your own.**

65. Interviewer: Do you have tendency to lie or steal?

You: There they go again! (**Remember the golden rule**). You are not in a confessional or are you?

66. Interviewer: What did your previous supervisor say your strongest or weakest points are?

You: You have just been given a life line. And that is an opportunity to praise-sing your skills relevant to the job. (But not to brag anyway)

67. Interviewer: Tell me about a time you didn't work well with your supervisor.

Caution!

You: An experienced applicant may not escape similar question to this one. As you already know, be positive in your response. You may recount an experience and the lesson you have learnt from it.

68. Interviewer: Do you smoke or drink?

You: Now, I wonder what that has got to do with them! Smiles... **(If it is not a tobacco or brewery industry job interview you are undergoing, I hope you will remember the golden rule.)**

69. Interviewer: What is the size of your suit?

You: I expect you know your size.

70. Interviewer: If our client slaps you, what would you do?

You: I sincerely hope you won't retaliate! Or would you?

71. Interviewer: What was the last or recent book you read?

You: (Rule no.3 will come very handy)

72. Interviewer: Tell me about your dream job.

You: If you mention Oil Company, military, banking industry for instance, whereas you are been interviewed for a teaching job; **this clearly shows a lack of interest on the**

prospective job. Do not be specific rather, try answer thus: a job that you will like what you do, the people you work with and always be eager to go to work. Think before answering that kind of question.

73. Interviewer: What motivates you to do your best on the job?

You: Finding pleasure in the job; sense of belonging, commendation and appreciation of your efforts and probably good incentive. How about that?

74. Interviewer: Can you list five words that best describe you?

You: Literate, competent, motivated, loyalist and team player. Or are you not? Smiles...

75. Interviewer: How long would you like to work with us if employed?

You: Being specific is not good! Something like this should work: I would like to work for a long time. Or as long as we both feel am doing a good job.

76. Interviewer: Explain how you would be an asset to this organization.

You: This is an opportunity to highlight your strengths and skills as they relate to the job.

77. Interviewer: Do you have trouble finding us?

You: no you don't.

78. Interviewer: What are you looking for in your next job?

You: You look forward to having more responsibilities and opportunities the prospective job will offer. (An experienced candidate may encounter such question)

79. Interviewer: Are you considering any other offer right now?

You: Even if you have got other offers, it is best to keep that to yourself and concentrate on the one you are being interviewed for.

80. Interviewer: Is there anything that will hinder you from starting work if employed?

Caution!

You: Nothing of course. And even if there is, please keep that to yourself for now.

81. Interviewer: What color of shirt are you wearing?

You: (Sounds "crazy" isn't? Smiles...) I had once been asked the above question as the very first question in a bank's job interview in the year 2010. And I smiled and mentioned the color of the shirt I wore which was white. So, I know exactly what am talking about here. And like I said earlier: expect any question.

82. Do you have any question for me?

You: Of course, you have questions. Please do not say no.

(**Apply rule no.2**). But this is not an opportunity to start asking how much you will be paid? When are you entitled to annual leave? When will you be promoted? And stuff like that, when you have not been given employment letter yet. **Rather, ask what basic qualities they desire in the applicants for the job? What will be your basic job functions if given the job? Who are you going to be working closely with if employed? There are several questions you can ask the interviewer at this juncture if given the opportunity and provided you did your home work well.**

83. Interviewer: Do you have trouble finding us?

Caution!

You: The interviewer wants to know if you are type that complains unnecessarily. **I just wish you would say no.**

84. Interviewer: What if your best friend borrows money regularly from the company's petty cash without returning it; and you have talked to him or her about it to no avail, what would you do?

Caution!

You: Of course, the company's interest comes first. You will report him or her to your supervisor. And that is just what they want to hear.

85. Interviewer: When can you start work?

You: Except you are still employed in your last organization, you can start even now except your employer decides otherwise.

86. Interviewer: What are you currently earning?

You: You are in better position to answer that if you are working before attending the interview.

87. Are you still employed in the organization listed in your CV?

You: I guess you know it is much easier to get another job while still working. Probably, this is one of the advantages of working experiences.

88. Interviewer: Have you ever taken the company's money with your colleague without your supervisor knowing and later replaced it?

Caution!

You: I am pretty sure that by now you know that the interview room is not a confessional.

89. Interviewer: How do you make important decision at work?

You: As a team player working with a view to achieving the set goals of the organization, you will seek the advice of colleagues before taking important decision in line with the organization's policies. Or don't you think so?

90. Interviewer: What will you do with your first salary?

Caution!

You: What is the interviewer's business? You would think! (Smiles...) Note that this is a tricky question sometimes asked towards the end of the interview with a view to discovering you attitude towards money and whether you have savings culture; plan and budget your money, or if you are the type that spends money recklessly and thoughtlessly and consequently live above your income. **A lady was asked the above question and she said she would spend it in a boutique. Needless to say she didn't get the job. Well, I hope you would save part of your salary for rainy day.**

91. Interviewer: How would you describe your personality to me?

You: This is another way of saying tell me about yourself. It is an opportunity to talk about your skills, experience, knowledge and abilities with relevance to the prospective job and the needs of your employer.

92. Interviewer: What makes you think that you are better than other candidates for this job?

You: Interviewers ask this kind of question to let you know that you are on a "hot seat" and that they mean business. **(Apply rule no.4)** whenever such question is thrown at you and do not make comparison with others applicants.

93. Interviewer: How would you describe your best friend and how you differ from him or her?

Caution!

You: Remember the golden rule while answering such

"double barreled question;" as it is believed that *in describing your best friend and how you differ from each other, an applicant may unknowingly reveal an earlier concealed weakness*! Remember the saying: show me your friend and I will tell you who you are? **Try to describe somebody your interviewer would be glad to employ.**

94. Interviewer: If you could change something about your personality, what could that be?

You: Note that this is another way of asking: what is it that you don't like about yourself? **Do not mention anything that can disrupt the progress of the job.**

95. Interviewer: What will your former employer or colleagues miss about you?

You: This is a golden opportunity to highlight your strengths.

96. Interviewer: Tell me how you have worked under pressure before. Or have you worked under pressure before? Or can you work under pressure?

You: Of course, if you have experience, go ahead and relate it.

97. Interviewer: If employed and you are given additional responsibilities other than your job functions without extra pay, would you do it?

Caution!

You: I just hope you would accept at this point in time. **Note that this may not be the case but possibly an "unpleasant"**

part of your job which the interviewer is trying to see how you would handle such situation.

98. Interviewer: I don't like your face! Or I don't like the way you are looking at me! Or why are you frowning at me?

Caution!

You: Don't be surprised if an interviewer begins to interview on this note by snarling "irrational" comments at you. Know that the interviewer has nothing personal against you but it is an intentional trick meant to discover your reaction if angry and how you would react to their clients or public in such circumstance. (**Do not frown but apply rule no. 4) Yes, smile and remain calm.**

99. Interviewer: Why are you thinking of leaving your current job?

You: An experienced candidate who is currently working may be asked similar question. **Do not say anything negative about your present job, boss or colleagues. So, stay positive. As such, you seek more responsibilities, and growth etc.**

100. Interviewer: You lack practical experience in this job. How would you cope?

You: Admit that you will need help and express your willingness to learn if given the opportunity.

101. Interviewer: How often do you visit your doctor?

Caution!

You: Visiting hospital regularly to the interviewer may mean that your health is failing. And as such, I just hope it's when you want to go for medical checkup or you are not feeling fine.

102. Do you have transport fare that will take you back home?

Caution!

You: Yes please. Even if you don't have, it would be in your best interest to keep it to yourself. The interviewers never kept money expecting that you won't have transport fare with a view to assisting you. **It is a trick meant to know whether you are an organized person who plans his or her activities or not.**

103. Interviewer: Would you have problem relocating, if transferred or posted contrary to your choice?

You: I sincerely hope you wouldn't!

104. Interviewer: Is there anything you forgot to tell me about yourself that you want to tell me now?

You: You have just been given another life line to reinforce why you are the best candidate for the job.

104. What is it that you don't like about your former job?

You: You wouldn't introduce negative impression or would you?

105. Interviewer: Tell me the kind of people you don't wish to work with.

You: You are a team player and can get along with people easily I presume.

106. Interviewer: Tell me about the last time you learned a new skill.

You: (Application of rule no.6 will help out)

107. Interviewer: If you were hiring a person for this job, what would you look for?

You: Be careful to mention qualities or traits that are needed and you have.

108. Interviewer: Are you willing to put the interest of the organization above yours?

You: I wish you would say yes.

109. Interviewer: Tell me about a failure you have had?

You: The aim of this question is to know how you dealt with the "failure" or "weakness" or "conflict" whatever it was. How did you overcome it? Did you ignore it? Did you learn anything from that experience? Bear this in mind while answering such type of question.

110. Interviewer: Do you have any question for me?

You: Sure, you should have some questions prepared in case you are given the opportunity to ask.

Wisdom Keys and Action Steps:

"The future belongs to those who see possibilities before they become obvious." **Ted Levitt**

"The wealth of your resources is limitless if you allow God to open your eyes to their possibilities." **Myles Monroe**

"Each day we need good thoughts to live by. And remember, you get what you order in life." **Alfred A Montapart**

"There is no limit to how far or how fast you can advance except for the limits you place on your imagination," **Brian Tracy**

"Once you start moving, keep moving. Don't stop. This decision, this discipline alone can make you one of the most productive and successful people of our generation." **Brian Tracy**

22

The Unwritten Rules in Summary

Finally, herein are the summary of the unwritten rules of job interview you should endeavor to familiarize yourself with before attending your next job interview if really and truly you want to secure a befitting job with all smiles and a class.

Rule No. 1 >>>> *Prepare and someday your chance will come.*

Rule No. 2 >>>> *If you are seeking employment in any corporate organization, it is important to have background* information about the organization's vision and mission and as well, familiarize yourself with general information about the organization.

Rule No. 3 >>>> Be an avid reader. Read voraciously and omnivorously. This will no doubt improve your communication skills and command of English Language.

Rule No. 4 >>>> Be bold, confident, composed, relaxed, SMILE and feel at ease whenever you are face to face with your interviewers.

Rule No. 5 >>>> Be in tune with current happenings. It pays off during job interviews.

Rule No. 6 >>>> Make a conscious and deliberate effort to be computer literate if you are not.

Rule No. 7 >>>> Know your strengths, abilities, skills, and talents and how to use them to your employers advantages if employed. And as a rule, do not mention any weakness that has direct bearing on the progress of the prospective job.

Rule No. 8 >>>> Have a role model and know some background information about him or her.

Rule No. 9 >>>> For no reason should you go into the interview room and sit down on your own volition without been asked to do so!

Rule No. 10 >>>> Dress corporate.

Rule No. 11 >>>> Obey the organization's instructions to the letter.

Rule No. 12 >>>> Manage you time efficiently and never be late for a job interview.

Rule No. 13 >>>> Speak simple and correct formal English Language. Avoid informal expressions or slangs; maintain good eye contact and body language.

Rule No. 14 >>>> Express your willingness to bring your past relevant experience to bear on the job if employed.

Rule No. 15 >>>> Simply do the "dos" and don't the "don'ts".

Rule No. 16 >>>> Never falsify credentials or give claims you cannot defend.

Rule No. 17 >>>> Use your knowledge of etiquette to distinguish yourself from the crowd.

Rule No. 18 >>>> Do not fear the interviewers but respect them. And as a rule, DO NOT argue or interrupt them if they are talking; let them finish before you talk. Otherwise, you will only succeed in disqualifying yourself from the exercise.

Rule No. 19 >>>> You have only first time to make first impression. Do not frown at your interviewers but always smile (though not unnecessarily) and behave well.

Rule No. 20 >>>>. The golden rule is: never introduce any negative impression throughout your interaction with the interviewers.

23

Expert's Helpful Comments

HEREIN, are some helpful comments from seasoned interviewers and recruiters that will guide you and clarify some specified and very crucial aspect of job interview questions generally:

Cruise

People have to understand that interviewers have heard pretty much every possible answer to their questions. Your bet *is to be honest,* because honest answers always come out sounding better than the answers they want to hear. Another key thing is that you have to be upbeat in an interview, **be excited that you are there and always keep a positive attitude.**

Don't answer every question right of the bat because even if you are not lying, it will come out sounding fake. **Body language also depicts a lot in an interview.** If you answer a question and use your hands, a slight shift of your body and tone of voice as if you are answering with passion, the interviewer will concentrate less on your answer but rather more on your form and tone of response. You will come off that you are truly excited to be there and that you want to engage the interviewer in your answer so they could feel what you are feeling. **Key thing here is not to sound like everyone else, be distinct; be honest.**

For all recruiters out there, keep in mind that the effective interviews are the ones where the interviewer tries to build a rapport with the interviewee and asks basic life questions as opposed to the standard questions because they know that they are not prepared for that type of interview so they like to see how you react and answer the questions. It's a good way to lead into an interview and then ask some of the more formal questions.

And remember 8 out of 10 interviews result with the interviewer asking if you have any questions for them, and you better, and they better be good ones that will make the interviewer think (you are interviewing them) about how to answer the question(s) thus, it reflects positively . Always go out of your way to look presentable even when not required and prepare a couple of days in advance, you will be surprised what a difference it will make.

One last thing, the question that will always almost arise in an interview is: "*Why do you want to work with us?*" Make sure you give a good answer because that question is the pivotal question of why you are there in the first place and it is usually asked at the beginning of the interview, so if you blow that one, the rest of the answers to the coming questions won't really matter.

Mike Perras

As far as been real goes, I have talked to a great many employers and believe me; they are tired of the template cover letter approach. Stir up, be real. It will be your edge. Take that real person and that edge to an interview. They may only see you for 20 minutes; you have got to make impression that lasts. Tell them what motivated you on your career path, that's a thinking person talking, not another template. *It's all about communication these days and not looking or sounding like everyone else. Be yourself, not who you think they want to see, when they see the genuine deal, it scores very well too.*

Ger

Hi, I work in IT and have interviewed many people. Apart from technical knowledge which is easy enough to measure, what I always looked for was someone I could work with on a day to day basis. *Somebody who appears confrontational or arrogant is doomed from the start.*

Be yourself, use common sense, and most importantly try to enjoy the experience. *Life is too short to be stressing about*

things which are really out of our control. I believe embracing the idea of failure as a learning experience takes away much of the anxiety and allows for much more natural expression, which I guarantee an interviewer will pick up to give you an edge over other applicants.

Anonymous Expert

I have been interviewing candidates for jobs. The biggest purpose of interview for me is to get a better sense of who each person is, and what their personality is like.

While you should put your best foot forward, I think the best approach ***is to be honest about whom you are.*** A lot of these questions don't have right answers, (although I suppose there are some really "wrong" answers).

A lot of these questions are different versions of "***Tell me about yourself.***" I read your resume, I know your last five jobs, so if I ask what are your strengths and weaknesses, I'm thinking about the role the job needs and how that will fit, but I'm also trying to get a sense of who you are as a person, and if you will fit in. As long as you don't say your weakness is drinking on the job or something, I think its ok. Refusing to respond seems a little weird and defensive to me.

I am trying to create a team, so it takes a balance of different personalities to make it work. If you fake it and still manage to get the job, I promise neither of us will be happy, and you will have to explain to your next employer why you got fired after six months.

Chris Sherret

Regarding the: **"What is your greatest weakness?"** question, there is an answer to this.

The principle is: Don't mention a weakness without knowing the solution. Everyone has weakness. To recognize this and have a solution is what makes the difference. Most people are lazy and not willing to go the extra mile to find an answer. Excuses don't get the job done.

Mike Perras

"***Can you describe your weakness?***" This is not designed to be a personal question at all. They are simply looking to see how well you can express yourself, as some people tend to look inside and it throws them off completely. Simple answer: "***Well, I used to have problem saying no to people, today I prioritize my day completely and in so doing I let my time management skills decide what I can truly say yes and no.***" Now, you have an answer that is in fact very personal and yet perfectly job related and in your answer you identified another attribute you have, time management skills, or at least you understand the term well enough to explain it. ***If your answer sounds sincere and genuine, you will score 10 out of 10 in any interview.***

I hired and mentored people for 30 years and today teach college students young and old what to expect in the job search process (cover letters, resume e.t.c). Your qualifications and experience get you the interview and that's all. ***Your interview skills will land you the job every time.***

Three16 is a Banker, Teacher, Broadcaster, Prolific Inspirational Writer and a Lawyer in the making. And can be contacted thru: **Three1620@gmail.com**

Job Interview Secrets!

In this book you will learn:

- The unwritten rules of job interviews

- The application of the rules in answering the toughest and trickiest job interview questions to your advantage

- Over 100 inescapable job interview questions and effective answering guides

- Professional advice by seasoned experts and authorities on job interviews

- And so many irresistible inspirational quotes that will challenge you to become visionary, think, dream big, set goals and of course, give you the push and driving force to achieve them!

www.ingramcontent.com/pod-product-compliance
Lightning Source LLC
Chambersburg PA
CBHW052324220526
45472CB00001B/266